Lyrical Enlightenment

Lyrical Enlightenment

FAIZA ZAMAN

RESOURCE *Publications* · Eugene, Oregon

LYRICAL ENLIGHTENMENT

Resource Publications
An Imprint of Wipf and Stock Publishers
199 W. 8th Ave., Suite 3
Eugene, OR 97401

www.wipfandstock.com

PAPERBACK ISBN: 978-1-6667-3465-2
HARDCOVER ISBN: 978-1-6667-9074-0
EBOOK ISBN: 978-1-6667-9075-7

11/03/21

Contents

Part 1

Crown

The Realm of Spirituality

Thoughts on the Prayer Rug

This is a flying carpet
Wooly threads levitate
Knot by knot
Unraveling aviation
In the face of the moon
Am I not a miniature bird?
Like an origami puppet,
fluttering left or right

I put my head down
My eyes close
And I see everything in nothing

The mysterious rug holds no barriers
Between the Creator.
My spirit's flight
Prayer travels me quicker
than the speed of thought
Towards eternal enlightenment

Crescent Phase

When the crescent moon appears
It is a blessing on the month of Ramadan
The impartial luminous silver
From the lunar calendar
Manifests the sky
A celestial blessing embodied in a thin curve
Or is it an ancient pagan symbol,
for those cusping their hands to Diana?
Or is it embodied by the curved sword
of middle eastern reign?
Through the midnight battles of Islamic conquest,

Only the crescent moon would know the answers
Watching the night through thousands of years
In times of peace and war
Those arched hands cupped together which sing prayer
Or hold the arched silver blade.

The Shepherd's Staff

Halt!
To the sight of the shepherd's staff
Who gathers infinite flocks

The universe is lost without the guidance of his thought

The world
would have been enslaved
By the madman
Who sits on the throne
If we were to have drowned,
Our blood would have become
the Red Sea

He holds the duality
Rod of direction,
Yet rod of the unknown.

The Compass of Faith

Mosques in the highway,
Temples in the mountains,
Sanctuaries in the city

The path to finding God
Should be easier than locating the building on a road map
The four sides of walls
Cannot confine belief
The four directions of a compass
Will not define intention
The rooftop is not sturdy enough to carry faith

Look inside,
The pedestal of truth
The pillars we follow
The ancestral voices chant
The eternal compass is guiding us

Cosmic Queen

I wear the necklace of planets
Chaining around my throat like galactic pearls
The asteroid belt wrapped around my waist
The sun, the golden Corona
the moon, the lunar mask
As the Milky Way curls streaming
Galaxies circling around my wrists
Astronomical bracelets
I am the cosmic queen
A celestial microcosm to the infinite dream
An expansion of both chaos and harmony

Black Hole Growth

And this very dark black hole continues to grow
A void in space continues to deepen
An empty vortex
A numbing midnight hollow
which submerges me deeper
Like the infinite expansion of space
Only to consume the entirety of matter
Only to cast into unbearable darkness

I began to dance again

Happy in the rhythm of joy
Twirling to the song of contentment
I began to laugh again
My giggles became tunes
bellowing into rings of ecstasy

I returned to myself
a happy free spirit again
They can never take the light
They can never burn a thousand candles in one blow

I carried the whimsical treasure chest miles to get where I am
when I opened it,
I unleashed the music of my soul

Emerging like rainbow stars
Glowing like luminescent fireflies
And to the sparks,
I danced

Part 2

Third Eye

The Realm of Awareness

Mental Hijab

The hijab of my mind
Protects my thoughts
From the glares of the ignorant
Wrapped in silks of patience
Pinned with wisdom
Neurologically complex wraps
of intellectual threads
Sewn by a crown of enlightenment

Why do you cover your thoughts?
Hiding the beauty of your mind
is a quiet game
I can tell behind your hijab
Your mind is a loud place

Ghost of Tragedy

Stuck to your breath
Like cigarette smoke
Invisibly wrapped
in the package of your lungs
Toxic treasure chest

The ghost of tragedy fuels uncertainty
that can't be seen at first
unwitnessed to the eye
Blowing like the counterclockwise wind
Microscopic dust

Who can see the phantom of sorrow?
Who whispers in the voice of depression?
A draining paranormal sighting
A superstitious disease
That no one believes in
Psychological cynics claim,
"It is not real"

Casting tricks on the mind
You try to wear a talisman to cure
The evil spirits in your mind
Trapped like a djinn
In a genie lamp

Sitting at the brain-shaman's office
Their P.H.D must hold black magic abilities
Clinical mysticism
over-the counter spells intended to heal

They think they know the wisdom to conquer chaos such as
The two headed monsters of north and south polar ends
"It's just a fragment of your dark imagination"
How do you explain what can't be seen to someone who thinks
they've seen it all?

Unrealistic

For all of those that get called unrealistic
Keep breaking someone's reality
Keep being innovative
Don't let anyone take your ideas from you
You have an idea you must protect it
You have a plan,
You must let it grow
Nurture it
For anyone that feels outcasted or misunderstood
You are more alike than what you know
Don't let feeling different
define you into not being a part of something bigger
That you must confine yourself into an image or role
that someone else has designed for you to play
I will keep trying you with my ideas
I am never going to lose faith
You will not make me feel hopeless or alone

A Collector of Flowers

I became a collector of flowers in a vase
Which all crumbled
And blamed myself
As the leaves decayed like winter forest
The browning call to the grave
Had I not cared enough?
I became self-aware of the mess I was planting
I am aware of my own nurturing

To Give My Perception

If I could give you anything in the world
It would be my perception of you
That way you could look at yourself through a conscience of confidence,
Instead of insecurity
Through a lens of self-love
Instead of hate
Through spectacles of acceptance
Instead of rejection

The Rising Sun is a Blessing

There are some places in the world,
where the sun rises
And midday it disappears
The sun is a blessing,
it is a glowing miracle
Truly feels the gratitude
the rays which feed us
Before it dips down, and you must wait a new day

Ode to Sight

Like love, sight is something experienced differently by everyone
Love is felt on varied altitudes and vibrations
Our vision became subjective,
Yet we made standards to measure
Colors, shapes, and sizes
Our perspectives can change
Maybe the eye doctor will argue
that my views are invisible

A Decade with No Roots

I count 10 years
I remember the spirit of my homeland
The first harvest of ripe mangoes from the trees of Punjab
The second times I count the two hands decorated with henna and
bangles
The third time of the three large pots stirring in the feast before a
wedding
The fourth which constitutes the four blocks away that you can
enter shops full of silk, lace, cotton, and net
The fifth which counts the rooftops with splashing water on sum-
mer days
The sixth which counts the six high mountains of Ziarat
The seventh which counts seven siblings passed down from my
grandmother
The eighth which counts the eight tandoori naans casting the
warm aroma
The ninth which comprises the nine rickshaws parked at the sides
of roads
10 years since I've stepped in home land of Pakistan
A decade with no roots

Part 3

Throat

The Realm of Communication

The World Became my Home

I am not east nor am I west
I'm not praised nor detest
Just human
I try my best
That the world became my home
Where my reflection in the mirror stares
Not knowing unaware
That the truth starts with me
I'm a wildfire
With my heart's desire
To burn like 100 pyres
I'm conflicted
By these opposing forces
By what society enforces
Where is my home?

The Canyon of Loneliness

In the canyon of loneliness
All is objective
You are cold but there is no snow
If someone has ever spoken out to the cliff
"This nothingness turned me into stone
I don't want your company
Or your false sympathy
No one understands my mentality
Or how I look at reality"

I'm not right or wrong
But please don't get mad at me
if I hurt your opinions
Because I'm losing my sanity
By the canyon of loneliness

Sometimes people mistake independence with loneliness
"I'm stuck with myself
I am my own help
Because everyone just goes and fends for themselves"

To survive, and stay alive
Cause another heart melt
Leaves a mark and it swells
You can't buy love it doesn't sell
All I can tell
The edge of loneliness has gotten me and myself

You can have the whole canyon become your audience
So why do you sit on your cliff alone?

Caravan of Truth

Take me with you
Desserts of honesty
Oasis of solitude
Ride upon the caravan of truth
The journey is within the reality experienced
But the destination resides
in silent realism
The world travels in the carriage of lies
Their coachman is a slanderer, gossiper, a driver of deceit
To ride the caravan of truth
Is a pilgrimage you must take alone
Your soul will navigate in the maps of intuition
Trust your inner GPS
Many devices track you to slow down your footsteps
When finding truth, you'll remove these shackles

Lessons After the Chaos

Some things you just can't bring back to life
Not after pain, suffering and strife
All this chaos and destruction

Realized the truth about existence
But I still try with persistence
To make the most of my condition
To not make the same mistakes
To end insanity and repetition
Never follow blindly in submission
No potion or prescription

Love and Forgive

Two words of wisdom
Intertwined to coexist

Without love you cannot forgive
Without forgiving you cannot love

Meditate to the silence of dual virtue
Close your eyes and detach for a minute

The past and the present are two different universes
If you enter the past, you go back to a different world
you will never become who you used to be
Change begins when I am in the present

I'm Tired of Living by Your Words

I'm tired of living by the words
Which you wrote with your sword-like pen
Inscribed by your own rules
In tight rolled parchment to confine me
Trapped pages freedom
No thinking spaces
Foretold by the scribble of your penmanship
And once I began to write my own story
the narration did not appeal to you anymore
My tale may not be perfect
But the work is my own

Won't Admit It

Some things are left better unsaid,
And spoken through action
I know deep inside there is a lot of love,
That you don't want to admit
Because you don't want to appear like others,
Whose names have been collected like paper strips scattered in a
glass jar
Whose stories can be picked up and read
However new chapters arise
When the time is right
All the truth will come
And pour like a fountain where bluebirds sing

Ode to Speaking

Since I first uttered my first words
To writing eloquent speeches
Language has continued to grow on me like trees with their leaves
extending
The queen of communication
The dukes of dialogue
The lords of linguistics
I studied the webwork of dialects
How is it we become our own omniscient orators

If I Look Up to the North Sky

If I look up to the North Sky
I know you will be glancing at the same stars
I know you'd be thinking of the same faded memories
That have been watched by the constellations that guide us
Because we were droplets under a celestial umbrella
The audience were comprised of the Zodiac
We made history on this earth
And the sky, the stars, and the moon were our witness

Witnessing It All Behind a Screen

I have witnessed all the madness in the world behind a screen
The magic of wifi allows me to access the earth from a metallic
rectangle
Now I can witness all the tragedies of mankind as an observer
From a glass casing which acts as a forcefield
And the borders which have restricted me
Come to life when I access the screen
And once I turn it off, there is nothing
Our ancestors would have been mystified by the workings of this
device
That connects so many people
But ultimately disconnects us from reality

Part 4

Heart

The Realm of Healing

Armor of my Heart

The world can condition
Someone with a life geared towards love
Into someone insensitive, aloof, and detached
Almost like a statue,
rocky heart with a stone face
Wearing an armor for their heart
Turning what they feel into steel
Building the Great Wall to blockade their territory
Protecting themselves from those who try to ambush them with
their feelings
Only allowing few to get through
If anyone

Nomadic

Everywhere I go
I say, "The world is my home"
Because now
I know there cannot be just one place meant for me
I have seen the
Pain and the suffering
After hurt and misused
Souls search for the universal truth
Found in the heart of you
Who ever knew?
To settle down with this nomadic heart
You've seen the Great Wall
But you have blockaded me from your heart
Built upon stones
Just so you won't fall
To settle down with this nomadic heart

Maybe the truth about forever
Is just a way to be distracted until they are gone
It is no guarantee
That love will set you free
When you have seen the whole world
While I lost it all
A wanderer a wanderer
Traveled afar
No sea can replace the floor of tears

Can a person become a destination?
To have waited all these years.
I want my home like shelter inside safe arms
Through the windows that stare past your scars
I've ended where I had to start

Fossilized

Don't get me flowers, jewelry, or gifts
Bring me the fossil of your love
Why fall in love
When we should dig for it
Timeless, deep, eternally valuable
Maybe a bit eroded
But hard to find
Yet unchanged, ancient, and permanent throughout the ages of the earth
It remains like sedimentary grains
Yet stays the same
Through floods and earthquakes
Pains and heartaches
This fossilized love we cannot break

Rocks collide in our interactions
Tectonic conversations

In Which World Is This?

When memories erase
These eyes which dismay
The Sun and moon meet
In which world is this?
Hope reaches the sky
The roads are easy now
In which world is this?
Ahead of poets
Behind are they?
Someone wakes up fictitious characters
In every story it is
Wiser than books
Get out of these pictures
In which world is this

Under This Umbrella

Under this umbrella
Hiding from the gaze of the world
Our faces eclipse beneath the nylon-fabric palm tree
As the sky sprinkles
To bless the moment
Why do we hide in umbrellas
knowing that the clouds have upset the sky enough to make it
weep

The Waterfall Will Not Flow

The rocks were built
Like towers of meteorite

To blockade cascades from falling
Strong barriers of an internal shield
The waterfall will not flow

Many spectate over Niagara Falls
To awe in the beauty of the infinite drops pouring
Further down
Further down

Vanished

Why have you vanished
Nowhere to be found again
Your existence may be here
But your spirit has disappeared
The hand of a friend
Is now an eerie ghost
Which floats with no amends
Ever since you've vanished
No call, no letter, no noise
Just the silent reminder
That I have lost importance for your existence
So why does it sting
to feel taken for granted
Am I warped with a
Parasitic attachment in the form of a spirit leech
I go about my days and nights
As I am trying to heal

Abandonment

It is so dangerous in this world
To wear your heart out in the open
Because if one has a heart of gold
you are a walking treasure chest
Which attracts the attention of
love-pirates, who try to rob you out of your admiration, care and compassion
Until you have nothing left to give
And leave your interior abandoned
To literally steal your heart and leave you misused,
taken for granted
Time was your currency
And you spent way too much time on them
To wear a heart of gold
Is a dangerous thing in this world
Because your love is something worth more than gold
And just because you are abandoned, you won't forever be alone

Mirroring Affection

When someone we love doesn't love us back
It shatters us like confused mirrors
It simply doesn't make logical sense
Don't we all wish to be loved
To mirror our own reflection
Onto someone that is not us

Ode to Breathing

My lungs are a miracle
My arteries are magical
The Vessels of converting the bronchial passageways flow
like an aerial river
I exhale
I inhale
What a beautiful phenomen
All because I breathe

What We Are Made of

You don't win someone's heart
We are made of flesh, blood and bone
The heart is not a trophy
It is not comprised of silver and gold
We give love
Not metals
But instead of earning one's trust
We earn coins
The currency of love is not to be founded in commerce
It is a trade which cannot be measured in coins
And it seems that we try to equate luxury with inner fulfilment

Part 5

Solar Plexus

The Realm of Power

Open Book

Stories written in someone's past
Inked with memories
Meant to last
Shelved away
By the narrator named Life
Who reads these stories silently
Entertaining the audience with honesty

Morbid Inspiration

What is inspiration?
You do not always need the light
Inspiration is dark
The moon cannot shine,
Without the black ink of the sky
Onyx comfort, opal-like hope
Ebony rays gleam
Inspiration is morbid
We search for angelic halos of light
In order to cover the vortex
Internalizing our souls
Used like bright band aids
Wrapped to cover horror
We live our lives inspired
By the final clock
The reality which every human must face
Ticking on numbers of light and dark

Freestyle

If I cause a calamity
Or if anyone is mad at me
It's their truth it is validated
They want to scream white lies
Cause honesty gets you hated
I broke free
Because I can't stay crated
I'm a wildfire
My image is a flat tire
I've got my ego deflated
But in a way I'm pumped up
And the heart it keeps racing
Like runners at the finish line
And the dreams it keeps chasing
Where you aim back with your mind's ammunition
Who's listening?
You say you're all ears
But what are you missing?
We're not even at intermission

What Sin is on Melanin?

You put me in a box to confine me
But what you say will never define me
I'll go places you'll never even find me
You talk about melanin
Like it's a sin
A shade of skin
The roots which are grown they are thrown in
One can win,
But never fit in
Not every skin tone can be adjusted like
Brewing tea leaves
As they seep into your cup
Setting the tone to how dark you please
Take pride in your own shade

Ode to Resilience

We can go through obstacles,
Thousands of times,
And still be victorious
Or we could fall over one hurdle,
And give up
Resilience is a choice,
Which determines,
Not if we cross the finish line
But if we are willing
To even endure the race
Until our thunderstruck
There was no rain
Don't Tell Me to Come Back
Tell a bird migrating,
Which left its nest to come back?
Tell a leaf,
Which fell from a tree to gravitate again
Tell a mummy to resurrect into the living
Don't tell me to come back
As easily as you let go of me
Just proved to me
That it's better to be loyal to your own dream
than a living nightmare

Bitter or Better

You decide to let it heal you
Or let it destroy you
From the pain that I can't explain
In words to throw you
Can't even get my soul to hollow
Can't even get the shots while I can't stop everybody knows which
I couldn't follow
Make it either bitter or better
Choice is up to you
Won't settle
for drowning in the past
To make false dreams last
No I don't want it back
Move forward and that is the best attack

Eating Grief

Eating grief
Silverware of sorrow
Platters of pity
Toasts made of liquid tears
I am eating grief
A buffet for pity party
A gathering of grief
In disdain and disbelief

can't consume all this sadness
How can I be eating so much that is in loss
They talk about being half-empty, half full
To look at the glass from perspective
But maybe from losing so much
It cleans up your stomach
A detoxifying digest
Grief is temporary
As I've looked beyond loss
Do not let it consume you

We Cannot Be Optimistic
When the Sun Is Shining

We cannot be optimistic when the sun is shining
You cannot be exclusive with optimism
We cannot use joy to cover up wounds
We cannot dismiss sorrow to shine the light on good times
We cannot be happy only when times are working in our favor
False positivity is a smile with a bandage covering it
Broken and absurd to look it
Rather we must be steadfast
To hold onto rays of hope
To understand that the storm shall pass
And when we endure through it,
we can understand that this is not the end
This will all pass

Part 6

Sacral

The Realm of Creativity

My Spirit's Tattoo

My spirit's tattoo
Permanently inked in the skin of my soul
Your colors pour to flow within my veins
Pure anesthetic to pain
Watercolors in my brain
Insane in ways which I cannot explain
Rationality sometimes decays
But creativity forever remained
Because your style is never replaced

Cranium of the Artist

Neurological landscape
Paint the streaks of my mind
Rainbow arrays of acrylic verbs
Brush my synesthesia
I hear pink
I taste blue
I touch orange
Sunset flavors
Starburst orchestra
Harmonize lyrical artistry
Cranium of the Artist.

The Sacredness of the Lotus

Untouched flora
Petals unfold
Lips of ripe nectar
Glisten like fresh summer fruit

They taste sweet
As the first bloom of cherry blossom
The sacredness of the Lotus
An earthly experience
Of nature's reopening
Every season cycles
Of birth, growth, maturity and death
Spring summer fall winter
Exist a sanctuary to be reborn

The Submission

The submission
The addiction
The prescription
The petition
You sign with your life away
The double sided pill that sinks in the glass
Bottle after bottle tossed in the trash
Injected, neglected, rejected
Over and over
The last thought was sober
Dragon breath in the air
Leaving behind children, goals
What's left to spare
Claiming life's not fair
Blinded by a grassy breeze
Rock candy that was never meant to eat
Tootsie rolls of nicotine
Cancerous factories
Rolls which fill empty holes
In the soul
Brought at the corner store
To feel whole
Lies to oneself once more
But what for?
Another trip?
It's not vacation

Queen of Fate

Let me be the queen of my fate
My reign is of my choice
What's a voice without a noise
My mind's open space
When you can't seem to recognize the fake
I wonder if I'm stuck
In life's masquerade

I have the right to amend
Sign the consent
Please don't mind
If I come across
As your prudent friend
Which I won't please
You expect me to breathe chains
When I walk free

The Cartographer's Device

Lift the pen
Make the sketch of your world
By your hands,
the earth forms
By your mind,
the seas flow
By your heart,
You crown the legend to the world's compass
What they erase on paper,
Is removed from our minds

Part 7

Root

The Realm of Trust

Beyond the Veil

In the darkest fabric of the night
All is hidden
Out of sight
The absence of light
People dream what it's like
Silent screams
Of what it's like
When the time was to fight
Tell me, what are you hiding?
Beyond that veil you won't ever show
That I won't ever know

They say they are hiding to survive
Because the boundaries a wildfire
The fight is on an incline
After the moon, there comes another sun

It Is to Protect You

"I have to put a mask of indifference to protect you" said X

"But why do you cover yourself" said Y

"I have to push you away to protect you" said X

"Why do you push the one's that care about you most" said Y

"I have to make you wait to protect you" said X

"The wait was never an issue. I'm always here if you need me" said Y

"I am not here to get you addicted to me like how gamblers get hooked onto jackpots" said X

"It's okay, we don't have to face down all our cards at once" said Y

"I want you to avoid me like how recovered alcoholics decline every drink" said X

"I do understand infatuation has intoxicating effects, but the realest form of love is truly a cloak of compassion" said Y

"I want your mind to stay sober from love" said X

"True love is witnessed sober, obsession is just a taste of drunkenness"

"It is a dangerous risk to dive in too deep" said X

"So then instead of diving deep, why don't we learn to fly? Flying sets you free. Diving too deep leads to drowning" said Y

"And I've listed the consequences and hung them at your door" said X

"I can handle the side effects of my choices" said Y

"Stay away while you can" said X

"Why don't you trust me" said Y

"Before you get attacked and trespassed onto the haunted territory" said X

"If we were to clash, I can handle the chaos, because it's you" said Y

"And you are on the ground defenseless because of what i did to you" said X

"Loving someone is not a weakness" said Y

"And my behavior enabled it." said X

"You are taking twice the weight of the responsibility and blaming yourself" said Y

"I have to scare you away to protect you from the demons inside me." Said X

"I wish I could help you. I'm not afraid, but now I feel pity. What monsters have you faced?" Said Y

Realization

I knew all along you did
It just hit you now
You were the river
But being the flow you emerged a waterfall
That let me knew how you hide how you feel
And you attach yourself to the other end of gravity

The Effects of Betrayal

Betrayal seems to be something
I repeat over in my head
Like the lyrics to a horrible song
Until I became used to the dreaded noise
Its tune screeches into my bones
Creating an unpleasant chill
A crescendo of ill-feelings
An orchestra of anxiety
Our minds synch to the beat of betrayal
Years later we hear that same song again
And remember those same emotions
And we walk down memory lane
Of the lyrics that have abandoned our minds
That awaken back to life
And somewhere in our ears the music just won't turn off

The Stranger I Became to Myself

I treated others like a stranger
When all along I was the stranger
to myself
Under a string of genuine pearls
To become someone who I was not
And the biggest actor was me
Who else would know the script of my pretentiousness?
When it was directed by me
A tale of imposter syndrome
I chased a dream in a race of external fulfillment
Only to realize what I wanted was in me all along
I dreaded the journey, for what?
To end up alone in this pyramid they have built
The apex is uncomfortable
The top is lonesome,
to sit on a throne by myself
The hard work and labor did not make me regret the effort
But it made me think
Was this the ending tale to what I imagined?
The scavenger hunt was more simple than I thought

Forgiving the Abandoner

Why do I tell myself
That the feeling of abandoned and loss can be forgiven
By those who have vanished like ghosts
How can I be mad at those who end it
How can I be mad at the dismissive friend who just doesn't care
It makes me want to shut myself off from the universe
For a person that nourishes themselves with love and kindness
Openly warming up and loving
The world walks like zombies and this reinforces me to change my
behavior
In order to walk amongst them
Or else they will eat me knowing I am human
That I have feelings and compassion
That is what makes us alive
And we shun our own speech to be confined and avoid the voices
of our own
In order to walk like the living dead amongst me
It leaves me spiritually disconnected
as we cut chords amongst each other

The Double-Sided Sword of Trust

Like a butterfly knife
One side trust
Other side betrayal
Go ahead and stab me
Try locating a new mark
In the map of my past try to find a new one
Either way we get hurt
Or we can learn to accept that trust fills in the blanks of our minds
Much like the butterfly knife that you clumsily hold to defend
yourself
Why are you afraid of trusting
When you alone hold the tool to your own pain
Trying to protect yourself

The Joke is on the Escapist

The joke is on the escapist,
Who never drinks the fountain of truth
Running away from reality like ants fleeing from water droplets
You will never be quenched until you face those floods
The satisfaction resides in overcoming the storm

Be Aware

Be aware of someone that has left you
And was never happy with you
To come back into another season of your life
And slander your name
With masqueraded lips
Because of resentment
That they never want to see you happy
Not with them, not with anyone
Because when had you, they had you under their influence
And once they cannot influence you anymore,
They influence those around you to sabotage you
When this happens, be aware
And if you run into them,
Make sure they see a big smile